Jess

SIMON AND SCHUSTER

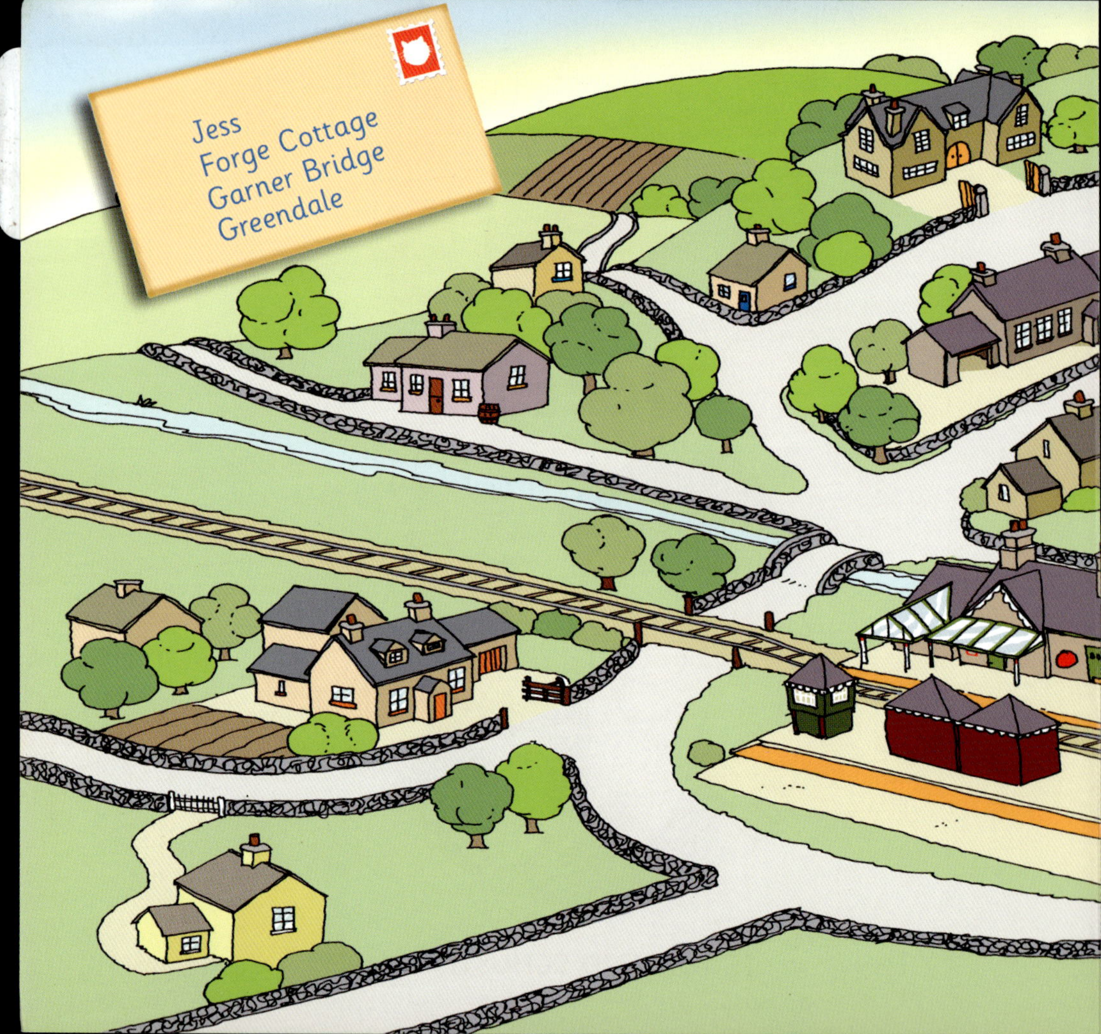
Jess
Forge Cottage
Garner Bridge
Greendale

GREENDALE

Come and say hello to Jess the cat!

Jess goes everywhere with Postman Pat. He loves to explore, sniffing out adventure in all sorts of unexpected places. The Greendale post just wouldn't be the same without him.

Post Office

Jess and Pat were on their morning delivery round.

“Parcel for you Reverend Timms,” called Pat.

“Aaah, the seeds I ordered!” smiled the Reverend. “Bless you both!”

Jess sniffed the parcel then nudged it with his nose. A brightly-coloured packet of seeds fell out onto the grass!

"Heavens, there's a hole in it!" cried Reverend Timms. "Well spotted Jess."

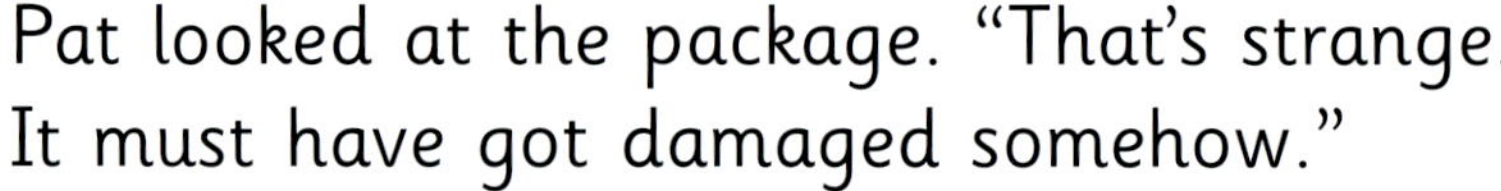

Pat looked at the package. "That's strange. It must have got damaged somehow."

When the Reverend opened it up, half the packets of seeds were missing!

"We'll get to the bottom of this I'm sure," said Pat. Jess nodded his head.

The next stop was P.C. Selby's house. The policeman was standing on his doorstep, looking very excited.

"You must have my new whistle!" he grinned.

"No, just a letter," said Pat, "looks like a bill I'm afraid."

"But the whistle should have got here three days ago," frowned PC Selby.

Jess twitched his ears. Something funny was going on.

Back at the Post Office, Jess started sniffing round while Pat asked Mrs Goggins about the missing seed packets and whistle.

"You won't find them here," she sighed. "All the mail was loaded into the van this morning."

Pat scratched his head. "I can't think where else to look."

Jess started to miaow, touching the window with his paw.

"Hmmm, looks like he's pointing towards the train station," said Pat.

Pat and Jess arrived just as the Greendale Rocket was puffing into the station.

"Hello there!" waved Ajay.

"Now I understand, Jess!" cried Pat. "You think the missing post has been left behind on the mail train."

But that wasn't what Jess meant at all. While Pat headed up to the platform, he decided to take a good look in the van instead.

Jess prowled round the heap of mail sacks in the back of the van. A funny smell had started to tickle his nose.

He gently prodded the pile, when suddenly one of his paws got stuck. No wonder the post had been going missing, the sacks were full of holes!

"Well done Jess!" cheered Pat when he got back. "These old mailbags must have got worn out."

Pat and Jess drove straight back to tell Mrs Goggins.

"What a relief that mystery is solved," sighed Pat. "I think we need a cuppa."

Jess shook his head. He leapt into the back of the van again, and started to creep towards the mailbags.

Pat couldn't believe his eyes when one of the bags moved!

Jess pounced.

Underneath the mailbag was a family of mice, sitting on a pile of nibbled letters.

"You've solved the real mystery Jess!" gasped Pat. "These little fellows must have eaten Reverend Timms' seeds."

Mrs Goggins came outside. "And look! The envelope's gone, but there's PC Selby's missing whistle."

But Jess couldn't take his eyes off the mice. He'd never got this close before!

That night Jess was treated to a fish supper.

"You're the hero of the day!" grinned Julian.

"And those mice will be much better off in Ted Glen's shed," said Sara.

Pat gave Jess a big cuddle. "Thank you. We make a great team."

Jess purred back as if to say, "the best"!

SIMON AND SCHUSTER
First published in 2005 in Great Britain by Simon & Schuster UK Ltd
Africa House, 64-78 Kingsway, London WC2B 6AH

Original writer John Cunliffe
From the original television design by Ivor Wood

A CIP catalogue record for this book is available from the British Library upon request

ISBN 1 416 90174 4
Printed in China

1 3 5 7 9 10 8 6 4 2